Every Girl Publishing
Publication date: December 5th 2018
Author: Sojourn Wallace
Email: everygirl@salamuk.org
Website: iameverygirl.org
Please direct all enquiries to the author

Every Girl Presents: Zimbabwe was based on a true story. While the events are true and people represented are real, some details may have been changed or dramatised to better suit our audience. While Every Girl does its best to keep each story close to the original storyline, this is not a biographical/autobiographical recount and was written in good faith by our team, as told by the original storyteller.

www.facebook.com/everygirlworldwide/
www.instagram.com/iam.everygirl/

Every Girl Presents: Zimbabwe

AGNES & ALL THE REASONS WHY

Sojourn Wallace

Bhumika Jangid

#refugeeswelcome

THIS BOOK IS DEDICATED TO ALL THE LITTLE GIRLS AND BOYS AROUND THE WORLD, STILL LOOKING FOR A PLACE TO CALL HOME. A PORTION OF THE PROCEEDS FROM THIS TITLE AND OTHER TITLES IN THE EVERY GIRL SERIES, GO TOWARDS PROJECTS THAT ADVANCE THE WELLNESS AND LIVELIHOODS OF REFUGEES.

A MESSAGE FROM JANE ELLIOT...

MY LIFE'S WORK AS AN EDUCATOR HAS BEEN TO SHOW THE UNIVERSAL TRUTH OF OUR CONNECTEDNESS AS HUMAN BEINGS AND HELP PEOPLE UNDERSTAND THAT THERE IS ONLY ONE RACE ON THE FACE OF THE EARTH, AND THAT IS THE HUMAN RACE. GOD CREATED HUMAN BEINGS AND HUMAN BEINGS CREATED RACISM. OF COURSE, ANYTHING YOU CAN CREATE, YOU CAN DESTROY, AND IT'S TIME FOR THE CREATORS TO DESTROY RACISM. IN AN EFFORT TO DO SO, I'VE SPENT THE LAST FIFTY YEARS TEACHING CHILDREN AND ADULTS THE VALUE OF TRUE EMPATHY, AS IT IS THE ONLY THING THAT ALLOWS US TO EXPERIENCE LIFE THROUGH ANOTHER PERSONS EYES; EMPATHY IS THE ONLY WAY TO CHANGE THE THINGS WE HAVE BEEN CONDITIONED TO BELIEVE.

TEACHERS CAN TEACH CHILDREN, AND SCHOOLS CAN SCHOOL THEM, BUT CHILDREN CAN USE BOOKS, INCLUDING THOSE NOT PART OF THE STANDARD CURRICULUM, TO EDUCATE THEMSELVES. IT IS MY HOPE AND BELIEF, THAT THIS SERIES WILL ENCOURAGE ITS READERS TO BECOME SELF-EDUCATING AND EXPAND THEIR KNOWLEDGE-BASE ABOUT THOSE WHO ARE DIFFERENT FROM THEMSELVES. CHILDREN WILL FIND A COMMON THREAD IN EACH STORY, WHICH WILL REMIND THEM OF THE JOYS, SORROWS, AND LESSONS OF THEIR OWN YOUTH. BY SHARING ONE STORY FROM ONE GIRL, FROM EVERY COUNTRY IN THE WORLD, CHILDREN WILL GROW UP MORE CURIOUS, MORE OPEN-MINDED AND BETTER PREPARED TO BUILD A WORLD WHERE EMPATHY AND JUSTICE ARE AT THE FOREFRONT OF EVERYTHING THEY DO.

-JANE ELLIOTT, EDUCATOR AND CREATOR OF THE BROWN EYE BLUE EYE EXERCISE.

LET'S DO IT TOGETHER

SKATE FOR REFUGEES

EACH EDITION IN THE EVERY GIRL SERIES, FUNDS THE COMPLETION OF A SPECIFIC PROJECT OR PROGRAM WITH OUR CHARITABLE PARTNER, SALAM U.K. FOR THIS EDITION, OUR MISSION IS TO BUILD A SKATEPARK + ROLLER DISCO NEAR THE SALAM HEADQUARTERS, IN LEBANON'S BEKAA VALLEY; HOME TO NEARLY 1.5 MILLION DISPLACED WOMEN, MEN AND CHILDREN. ONCE COMPLETED, OUR PARK WILL BE OPEN TO REFUGEE CHILDREN, AS WELL AS LOCALS, TRAVELLERS AND OF COURSE VOLUNTEERS LOOKING TO SHARE THEIR SKATING/SKATEBOARD EXPERTISE. TOGETHER WITH SALAM U.K., WE HAVE ALREADY RAISED THOUSANDS OF DOLLARS AND COMPLETED DOZENS OF PROJECTS TO SUPPORT THE HEALTH AND WELLNESS OF DISPLACED PEOPLE ACROSS THE GLOBE. THIS TIME, WE ARE VERY EXCITED TO HAVE OUR SKATE COMMUNITY INVOLVED !

ANY FUNDS RAISED UP TO $10,000 WILL BE MATCHED BY OUR FRIEND + LONG TIME SUPPORTER SUSAN SARANDON!

FOR REFUGEES. FOR LOCALS. FOR YOU.

iameverygirl.org/skatepark

ABOUT EVERY GIRL

EVERY GIRL IS DEDICATED TO SHARING THE BEAUTY & DIVERSITY OF WOMEN FROM ALL WALKS OF LIFE. WHAT STARTED OFF AS A CHILDREN'S BOOK, IS NOW A GLOBAL MOVEMENT AND HAS ALREADY REACHED OVER ONE HUNDRED COUNTRIES WORLDWIDE. FROM OUR HEADQUARTERS IN LONDON, WE TRAVEL FAR AND WIDE TO PROVIDE A PLATFORM FOR WOMEN AND GIRLS TO HAVE THEIR STORIES HEARD.

EVERY GIRL IS THE WORLD'S FIRST AND ONLY CHILDREN'S BOOK TO TELL ONE STORY, FROM EVERY COUNTRY IN THE WORLD! OUR MESSAGE IS ONE OF LOVE AND UNITY; AND WE AIM TO ENCOURAGE THE NEXT GENERATION TO BECOME CURIOUS AND EXCITED TO LEARN ABOUT PEOPLE WHO COME FROM DIFFERENT BACKGROUNDS THAN THEIR OWN. A PORTION OF OUR PROFITS ARE PUT TOWARD REFUGEE WELFARE PROGRAMS IN LEBANON'S BEKAA VALLEY.

OUR PARTNER

SALAM LADC UK (SALAM UK) WAS ESTABLISHED IN JANUARY 2017 BY INTEGRATING OFF TRACK HEALTH INTO THE NETWORK OF SALAM LADC. OFF TRACK HEALTH WAS FOUNDED IN 2015, TO PROVIDE MEDICAL ASSISTANCE IN RESPONSE TO THE OVERWHELMING NEEDS OF REFUGEES ARRIVING ON THE GREEK ISLAND OF LESVOS. SUPPORTED BY A LARGE COMMUNITY OF VOLUNTEERS AND WITHOUT PAID STAFF, OTH OFFERED 24/7 MEDICAL AND DENTAL SERVICES, TREATING 250 PATIENTS/DAY. ASSESSMENTS OF OTHER COUNTRIES AFFECTED BY THE REFUGEE CRISIS AND RECENT NATURAL DISASTERS, HAVE TAKEN THE OFF TRACK HEALTH TEAM TO HAITI AND LEBANON'S BEKAA VALLEY, WHERE THEY PARTNERED WITH SALAM LADC.

THE SALAM NETWORK PROVIDES FLEXIBLE, EFFECTIVE, AND NON-BUREAUCRATIC ASSISTANCE, AIMED AT STRENGTHENING INTER-COMMUNITY DIALOGUE, AND ASSISTING THE MOST VULNERABLE POPULATIONS IN LEBANON.

YOU ARE IN SOUTH EAST AFRICA

GET IN MY BELLY

Sadza: This is the most common dish found in Zimbabwe and is a stiff maize meal that is like a thickened porridge.

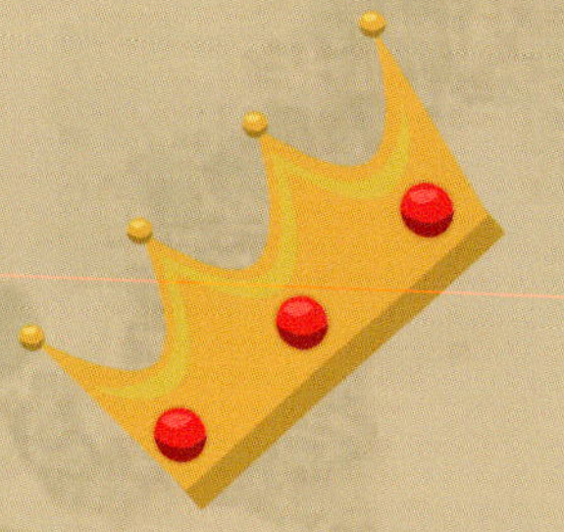

WATER HERE, THERE, EVERY WHERE

Zimbabwe contains lots of bodies of water, great and small, including the Zambezi and Limpopo rivers.

THE FALLS

One of the largest waterfalls in the world, Victoria Falls, is located on the Zambezi River. It is wider than a kilometer and has a height of more than one hundred meters.

NEIGHBORLY LOVE?

Zimbabwe shares its borders with Botswana, Zambia, Mozambique, South Africa and Namibia.

KEY FACTS OF ZIMBABWE

- Capital and largest city: Harare
- Official languages: 16 languages
- Population: 16,150,362 making it the 73rd largest country.
- Currency: United States dollar
- Roads: People must drive on the left.
- National sport: Football/soccer

IT'S A BIG ONE!

Zimbabwe became independent from the United Kingdom on April 18, 1980. In terms of land area, Zimbabwe is three times the size of England.

Zimbabwe

"Why do I have to go to bed?"
"Why do I need to eat my vegetables?"
"Why this...why that?"

Some kids are always asking why. Unfortunately for my mother, I was one of them. My mother would say, "Agnes, go to the market and get me a carton of milk."

But I didn't like walking to the market. It was hot on the path to the market. There was no music on the way to the market. And then there were the cows. Oh, those big, ugly cows lining the roads. Absolutely terrifying! So instead of saying "O.K. Mama", I would ask..."Why?"

This would send my mother into a frenzy! You see in the Shona culture it's considered rude for a child to "question" an adult, especially if the question is why. In fact, mother once told me that a child who asks why was not a child at all, but rather a form of punishment for bad deeds she committed in a previous life.

"Because I said so! She snuffed. Now off you go!"

Not brave enough to ask her "why she said so," the conversation usually ended with me disgruntled, slowly dragging my feet up the hill to the market; only running when I saw the ferocious wild cows.

In general, it seemed as if my questions were met with resistance by everyone; aunts, uncles, even the man who swept the streets. If it wasn't a dismissal, the person would simply reply with a lesson from the Bible, backed up by scriptures that didn't exist.

"You know Agnes, the Bible says that the rod is only spared for the child who does not ask why," or "Honour thy mother and father by providing peace and absence of questions." Eventually it seemed the whole Bible had been written to keep me from becoming the smartest person of all time.

Lucky for me, there was one place, or rather one person, whom I could bring my mountain of questions to. All my hows, whats, whens, and especially my whys, were all welcomed by my best friend Lorde. Lorde was truly the best. She was short, round with beautiful white curls that would shape-shift from one moment to the next. She was also one of the most respected elders in my community, so knowing she liked me, gave me a veil of confidence. Each day on my way home from school, I would stop by her house to chat.

'Lorde, why do you think the president looks like a crying frog?' I asked one afternoon.

'Well Agnes, rumor has it he's actually a toad. Like my hair, he shape-shifts.'

'Lorde, why is my hair black and your hair white...I bet you'd look great with black hair!

'Ha! I'm lucky to have any hair at all. I'm nearly two hundred years old!'

'Two hundred?!'

'Well, seventy-nine to be exact - but yes, almost two hundred.' She said with a cackle, then on and on we'd go.

I loved Lorde's hilarious answers to all my questions. Each time we met, I would leave with the biggest smile on my face.

That evening, when I left Lorde, I was surprised to find a man looking inside the window of our neighbor Amira's house. I knew everyone from our town, and he didn't look familiar, so I was sure he must be lost.

'Excuse me, sir, are you lost? Because I am from here and I know where everything is and I-'

Before I could finish my sentence, he looked at me and went frantically running in the opposite direction as fast as he could. Worried he may get even more lost, I decided to run after him.

'Sir, sir, wait! I can help if you follow me.' I shouted. 'I know where the market is and the best route to avoid the cows! Just wait!'

But the man kept running. Eventually, he got so far down the path, I could no longer keep up. I must have frightened him, I thought. I'd had lots of reactions to my questions, but never anyone run away from me. With my head hanging low, I decided to make my journey home. That evening, I told mother about how I'd scared the poor man.

'Did he say anything else before he ran away? Did he ask you to come with him? How old did he look? Are you sure he wasn't from here?' She badgered on. 'Was he carrying anything? How tall was he? How short was he? Did he speak Shona or Tsonga?' On and on she went, asking more and more questions about the man's appearance. It seemed she had missed the point, and now because of me, he may be lost forever.

'Never mind,' I told her. 'I'm sure he will find his way home eventually.'

The next morning, just as I was ready to set off for school, mother stopped me in my tracks.

'Agnes, when you get out of school, come straight home. No stops, no time at the park, no playing outside. No questions asked. Straight home. Do you understand?'

Mother stood in front of me with her hands on her hips, one eyebrow raised and a look so serious, I knew she meant business. But, I couldn't help her with her business. I couldn't even help myself. It was as if the words spoke themselves and I was just in the passenger seat as my heart spoke:

'But...'

'Agneeees...' Mother said with a warning.

'But...but... whhhhhy?'

'Because I said so!' She said, unsurprisingly losing her cool.

Also unsurprisingly, mother returned home from work to find me in the field, jumping rope and singing songs as if the conversation never happened.

'That's it, Agnes! I can't take it anymore! We're going to talk to Lorde! She's the only one you seem to listen to.'

'Oh no, not Lorde!' I pleaded.' If she knows what I've done, who will I talk to then?'

Mother took hold of my hand and lead me through the field that separated Lorde's house and ours. I did not want to go, and as she urged me along, I shifted between acting like I was a large wooden plank and a frantic octopus, squirming to get free.

My efforts failed me of course, and once we arrived at Lorde's house, mother began telling her side of the story from the day's events.

'Then she said why! Oh Lordy, Lordy! Because I said so, that's why I told her...and then again, she said why! Ey! This child! This child, this child. She's going to send me to an early.' Mother cried, all while waving her hands to the ceiling and calling out to the heavens. Finally able to catch her breath, she looked to Lorde.

'Lorde, please fix this child or ask Jesus on my behalf!' She cried.

Lorde sent a smile in my direction, then gave mother a reassuring nod to let her know she'd come to the right place. Slowly, Lorde pushed herself up from her chair, then took the floor to give her "wise" speech like any good elder would do.

'Agnes, my dear. Sometimes asking why is great! It helps the mind to grow and encourages the spirit. But sometimes, we must trust those who care for us when they tell us something. Even if that something, is something we do not want to hear. You were told to stay inside because there are strangers in the area who may be up to strange things.'

'Strangers?' I asked.

'Yes, strangers. So before you go back outside, we need to make sure these people are good people. That's why next time Agnes, you should just say "OK".'

I looked at mother, then at Lorde. Back and forth my eyes bounced between them as I tried to untangle all that had been said. It was all starting to make sense. Maybe the man at the window wasn't afraid of me. What if I hadn't scared him at all. In fact, perhaps he was the stranger up to strange things! I stayed silent for a moment, but then it happened. That very moment, for the first time, I said...those words.

'OK, Mama. OK, Lorde.'

Together they gasped and mother froze as if moving would undo the moment.

'Well... Agnes. Thank you,' mother said. 'That is very nice to hear!'

'Yes, Agnes. Good girl!' Lorde congratulated, then together they let out a sigh of relief.

'....but am I allowed to go outside tomorrow?' I asked.

WHO WE ARE

SOJOURN A. WALLACE - AUTHOR

SOJOURN WALLACE IS THE CREATOR AND AUTHOR OF THE EVERY GIRL SERIES. SO FAR, SHE HAS PUBLISHED 12 ORIGINAL CHILDREN'S STORIES AND CO-AUTHORED THREE OTHERS; INCLUDING THE BEST SELLING TITLE 'MILO GOES TO MARS' BY ABI ESMENA. ORIGINALLY FROM LEXINGTON KENTUCKY, SHE HAS LIVED IN SEVEN COUNTRIES WORLDWIDE AND CURRENTLY CALLS LONDON, ENGLAND HOME. SOJOURN HAS A B.A. IN FINE ARTS AND A M.A. IN INTERNATIONAL RELATIONS.

BHUMIKA JANGID - ILLUSTRATOR

BHUMIKA IS AN ILLUSTRATOR HAILING FROM RAJASTHAN, INDIA. AFTER FINISHING HER STUDIES, SHE WORKED AS A GRAPHIC DESIGNER AND EVENT UALLY CAME TO REALISE THAT HER TRUE PASSION WAS IN ILLUSTRATIONS, CHARACTER DESIGN, AND CARTOONING. UPON THIS DISCOVERY, SHE LEFT HER JOB AND BEGAN TO LEARN MORE ABOUT HER PASSION. SHE IS NOW HAPPILY WORKING AS A FREELANCE ILLUSTRATOR.

COMPLETE THE SERIES AT IAMEVERYGIRL.ORG
Every Girl Presents: Zimbabwe
Agnes & All the Reasons Why
Every Girl Presents: Iceland
Margrét & The Elves of Iceland's Second Realm
Planet Roller Skate
Milo goes to Mars
Every Girl Presents Morocco & France: A Multicultural Edition
Myriam & the Bridge Between Two Worlds